IDIOMS 1

by VERA McLAY

Funny pictures: John Bianchi

Editing: Howard B.Woods
       Michael Sutton
       Cornelius von Baeyer
       Christine Deeble

Based on original material by Robert Courchêne

Copy Editing and Design: Edith Pahlke

Spanish translations by Norma Fernandez of
the Canada-Mexico Exchange Program

Thanks for assistance with French and
Spanish translations to Susan Anderson,
Vivianne Henriquez, Marc Lebel, Guy Roy

A **tape** of all the situations (including the
appropriate idioms) is also available.

For information on Language Training Canada's
materials for teaching English and French as
second languages, please contact:

       Course Development Directorate
       Language Training Canada
       Public Service Commission of Canada
       15 Bisson Street, Room 219
       Hull, Quebec
       Canada K1A 0M7

INTRODUCTION

TO THE STUDENT

The purpose of the IDIOMS modules is to introduce you to common idioms and proverbs in spoken English.

Each module contains 15 sections each with 10 idioms and appropriate contexts grouped under topic headings. For instance 10 time-related idioms like 'It's high time' are listed in Section 1 — Time Expressions. You have to choose the appropriate idiom to fit the contexts given in each section. You will often be able to decide which idiom is appropriate from the context itself. However, for each context we have also supplied (Canadian) French, Spanish and non-idiomatic English equivalents. Where possible the French and Spanish equivalents are idiomatic. Where an idiomatic equivalent does not exist we have given translations and paraphrases.

IDIOMS is designed to be self-instructional. You can work through each module section by section, or you can simply choose the topics that interest you most and do only those sections. If you decide to pick and choose sections on your own, you may find that some of the contexts contain idioms you are not familiar with because some of the idioms introduced in earlier sections are re-utilized later.

When you have completed a section you should check your answers against the answer key at the end of the book.

For those of you who work through the sections in sequence, we have supplied a test after each five sections to let you see how many idioms you have learned. You may even want to do one of the tests before you do any of the sections to see whether you already know these idioms.

As you are already aware, a knowledge of idioms is essential for understanding spoken English. People use them all the time in place of more formal ways of expressing themselves. Idioms add life and vitality to language. Without idioms language may be correct, but tends to be rather dull.

If you wish to study idioms for recognition purposes only, then you need only work through the module as we have suggested. On the other hand, if you want to be able to use these idioms when speaking English, then you will have to practise using them as often as possible.

When you are speaking it is important that you use the correct idiom in the appropriate situation. For example, some idioms are used mainly in informal situations while others are appropriate in both informal and formal contexts. Most of the idioms in these modules are appropriate for general use. However, some idioms like 'Get a load of _____', 'Turns me on', and 'So what?' should be used mainly in informal contexts.

We have tried as much as possible to give you an indication of the kind of situation in which each idiom is likely to be used by providing fairly lengthy contexts. These contexts range from typical street situations to many that involve office-talk — conversations that are often heard in business or government. It is, of course, impossible to give you all possible uses of all of the idioms. It is up to you to extend the range of your use of these idioms by listening to how they are used in conversations, on television and radio, and in movies.

Whatever way you decide to use IDIOMS we hope you enjoy them.

TO THE TEACHER

The IDIOMS modules contain common English idioms selected for their frequency and usefulness in up-to-date spoken usage in North America. The situations in which the idioms appear are in authentic conversational English, many of them set in general business or government environments. The booklets are intended mainly as self-study workbooks for ESL students but there are many ways for a teacher to use them. Students may be assigned to study sections on their own or under the teacher's guidance. The dialogues in each exercise have been recorded for class practice in listening comprehension.

The style of the dialogues is in many cases quite informal. In fact many different registers are represented in the dialogues, and teachers should act as guides pointing out which idioms are appropriate to which registers and situations. In addition to developing the listening skill students can practise idioms by writing their own situational dialogues or by role playing around the meaning of an idiom.

TABLE OF CONTENTS

For your convenience, the lists of idioms at the beginning of each Section are also presented on the back cover.

SECTION 1

Time Expressions

a. right off the bat
b. every now and then
c. it's high time
d. once in a blue moon
e. just in the nick of time
f. in no time flat
g. in the long run
h. on the double
i. for the time being
j. out of the blue

Fill in the blanks with the best idiom from the list above. Use the equivalents below each context in making your choice.

1. "I hear you've given up downhill skiing."
   "Not completely. I still go _____, but I'm much more interested in cross-country skiing and snow-shoeing. And besides, there aren't any line-ups for tows and chair lifts."

   de temps en temps; de temps à autre   *de vez en cuando*   *from time to time; sometimes*

1

2. "Hi, Pete. I see you're still driving that old wreck. I thought you were going to buy a new car."
"I am. I'm getting a new one next week but I'm going to lease it."
"Really? Isn't that more expensive than buying it?"
"No, _____ it's actually cheaper to lease a car than to buy one."
"How do you figure that?"

à la longue	*al fin y al cabo; a la larga*	*in the end; in the final result*

3. "I hear you had a pretty rough weekend."
"Yes, it's lucky we didn't lose our kids."
"What happened?"
"We went shopping and left the iron on.
It short-circuited and set the kitchen on fire.
We arrived _____
to save the kids."
"Were you ever lucky."

juste à temps;
juste au bon moment

justo a tiempo

at the last possible second

4. "Morris, the boss wants to see you in his office right away."
"O.K. I'll be there in a couple of minutes. I just want to finish this letter."
"You'd better forget the letter and get in there _____ . You
know he hates to be kept waiting."

au plus vite; *sur-le-champ*	*en seguida;* *inmediatamente*	*fast; quickly*

5. "What beautiful flowers."

"Thank you. My husband sent them for our anniversary."

"Lucky you. I love flowers but I have to buy them for myself. My husband only sends me flowers
_____ . He can't even remember the date of our anniversary."

"Well, nobody's perfect."

très rarement;	*muy de vez en cuando;*	*rarely*
une fois dans cent ans	*cada año bisiesto*	

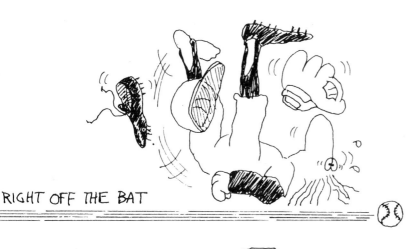

RIGHT OFF THE BAT

6. "I wish Jack was here."

"Why?"

"This tape recorder is making a funny noise and I need it right away. The last time this happened
Jack fixed it _____ ."

"Let me have a look at it. I may not be as fast as Jack but I can probably fix it."

"Sure. Go ahead."

en un rien de temps;	*en un minuto;*	*quickly*
en un tournemain;	*al instante*	
en un tour de main		

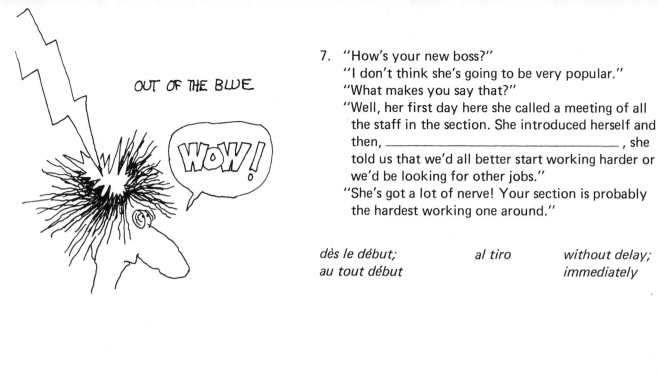

OUT OF THE BLUE

WOW!

7. "How's your new boss?"
"I don't think she's going to be very popular."
"What makes you say that?"
"Well, her first day here she called a meeting of all the staff in the section. She introduced herself and then, _____ , she told us that we'd all better start working harder or we'd be looking for other jobs."
"She's got a lot of nerve! Your section is probably the hardest working one around."

dès le début;   *al tiro*   *without delay;*
au tout début   *immediately*

8. "Hey, Sue. I've just heard our department's moving to that new building on Laurier. Is it true?"
"It seems to be. The boss announced it at our section meeting this morning. I hope we move soon. I'm sick of these so-called temporary buildings."
"Yeah. _____ we moved. These old barracks are falling apart.

il est grand temps   *ya es tiempo;*   *it's long overdue (that)*
                               ya es hora

9. "Did you hear that Brian is leaving his wife?"
"Who told you that?"
"He did. We were having coffee this morning and _____ he announced that he and his wife are breaking up. He didn't say too much but I gather there's a third person involved."

tout à coup;   *de repente*   *suddenly without warning;*
soudainement   *unexpectedly*

4

10. "Mr. Stuart in room **411** is asking if he can be released from hospital tomorrow, doctor."
    "I'm afraid not, nurse. We want to run some more tests on him. I'd rather keep him here
    _____ ."

pour le moment;   *por el momento*   *temporarily; for a short time*
pour un certain temps

Answers on page 83.

5

SECTION 2

Being Confused or Distracted

a. slipped my mind
b. I haven't got a clue
c. can't make heads or tails of
d. on the tip of my tongue
e. don't know which end is up
f. beats me
g. I've lost my train of thought
h. racking my brains
i. couldn't get a word in edgewise
j. are over my head

IT SLIPPED MY MIND...

Fill in the blanks with the best idiom from the list above. Use the equivalents below each context in making your choice.

(Mary and Alice are talking)
Mary: "What we really need is a new approach to work. I was thinking ab . . ."
Jack: "Hi Mary. Did you have a nice weekend?"
Mary: "Not bad! And yourself?"
Jack: "Can't complain. Can't complain."
Alice: "What were you going to say?"
Mary: "I can't remember. With Jack interrupting me, _____."

j'ai perdu le fil   *se me fue el hilo;*   *I forgot the idea I was talking about*
                                   perdí el hilo

6

2. "Tom, what's the capital of Yugoslavia?"
   "Don't ask me. _____ . You know I'm hopeless at geography."

   je n'ai pas la moindre idée   *no tengo la menor idea*   *I have absolutely no idea;*
                                                                            I have no answer

3. "Have you managed to assemble the bookcases yet?"
   "I'm afraid not. I've been studying the plans for the last hour but I _____
     them. I read the French instructions too, but that confused me even more."
   "Let me have a look. Two heads are better than one."

   je n'arrive pas à les démêler   *no entiendo nada;*   *I can't understand them*
                                          no puedo
                                          descifrarlo

4. "Well, did the boss approve your request for extra man-years?"
   "Are you kidding? The minute I hinted at extra staff he started talking about budget restrictions,
     man-year cutbacks, overspending in other sections — he went on and on for at least an hour. I tried
     to interrupt a couple of times but I _____ . After a while I just
     gave up and left."

   je n'ai pas eu la chance   *no pude decir ni jota*   *didn't have a chance*
   de placer un mot   *to say anything*

5. "O.K. guys, we're off. Red Lake here we come."
   "I hope we didn't forget anything important. Did you remember to pick up the booze, Jack?"
   "Oh no. It completely _____ ."
   "Are you crazy? How could you forget the most important thing for a fishing trip?"
   "It's not too late. Where's the nearest liquor store?"

   cela m'est sorti de l'idée;   *se me pasó por completo;*   *escaped my memory;*
   cela m'a échappé   *se me olvidó*   *I forgot (it)*

6. "Quick. Terry. What's the name of the guy who gave the talk at this morning's session?"
   "Gee, let me see. It's an unusual name — Polish I think. Kowalski?   No it's not that, but it's
   close. That's annoying. It's _____ but I just can't get it out."
   "Oh-oh! He's coming over here, and I want to ask him to give a talk at our next training session.
   It looks bad if I can't remember his name."

   je l'ai sur   *lo tengo en*   *something I can*
   le bout de la langue   *la punta de la lengua*   <u>*almost*</u> *remember*

7. "What's up, Joe? Your door is always closed. I've been trying to get in to see you for two days. Your secretary says you're not to be disturbed."

"It's this new computerized, financial information system. For the last two days I've been studying the print-outs until my head's spinning and I still can't understand them. I'm thoroughly confused. In fact I _____ anymore."

"I know what you mean. Computer print-outs do the same to me."

je n'y comprends   *ne sé que hacer*   *am totally confused*
plus rien

8. "How come the new photocopier isn't working?"

"Don't know. (It) _____ .
The repairman just left fifteen minutes ago and said it was working fine."

"I know how to make it work. How about plugging it in."

je ne comprends pas

no lo entiendo

I am uncertain;
I don't understand it

I HAVEN'T GOT A CLUE...

9. "How's your computer course going?"

"I'm not really sure, to tell you the truth."

"What do you mean, you're not sure?"

"Well, I understand the manuals — at least I think I do — but I don't understand half of what the prof talks about. He uses too many technical words. I'm afraid his lectures _____ . Maybe I should have taken the introductory course."

sont trop difficiles pour moi;   *son demasiado difíciles para mí*   *are too difficult for me*
me dépassent

10. "What are you scratching your head for?"

"I've been _____ all morning trying to remember the name of the company that gave that course in Transactional Analysis. I know it's a Toronto company and the name's on the tip of my tongue but I just can't remember it."

"Why don't you look it up in the files?"

"'Cause I can't remember what I filed it under."

je me creuse la tête   *devanando los sesos;*   *I've been thinking hard*
                                quebrando la cabeza

Answers on page 83.

IT'S ON THE TIP OF MY TONGUE!

SECTION 3

Knowing or Agreeing

a. on the same wave-length

b. knows the ropes

c. put your finger on it

d. straight from the horse's mouth

e. put two and two together

f. rings a bell

g. see eye to eye

h. heard it through the grapevine

i. took the words right out of my mouth

j. knows it like the back of his hand

Fill in the blanks with the best idiom from the list above. Use the equivalents below each context in making your choice.

1. (Two close friends.)
   "How's married life treating you?"
   "Pretty good."
   "Now that the honeymoon's over have you had any fights?"
   "Not really. We sometimes disagree on small things but we usually _____ on the major issues."

   *voyons les choses
   du même oeil*   *estamos de acuerdo;
                                       concordamos*   *agree*

2. "Hey, Jill. Does the name 'Ladouceur' mean anything to you?"
   "Ladouceur. Let me see . . . um . . . That name _____ but I just can't place it."
   "I've got this message on my desk to call him but I don't know who he is."

me dit quelque chose   *me suena*   *sounds familiar*

3. "How are you getting along with your new supervisor?"
   "Just great. He's got some really modern ideas about how to organize the work. He's got us on flexible hours and has promised us a really effective career development program. In fact, he's doing all the things I always said we should be doing."
   "Sounds like you two are _____."
   "Right, we're going to make a great team."

sur la même longueur d'onde   *hablando de lo mismo; en la misma onda*   *having the same sort of ideas*

4. Bob: "Harry, have you got your map of the park?"
   Harry: "Sorry, I left it in the car."
   Peter: "No problem. Jack grew up in this area and he _____."

le connaît comme le fond de sa poche   *lo conoce como la palma de su mano*   *knows it extremely well*

5. "Hey, have you heard the latest? Old Smith is leaving."
   "That's too good to be true. Who told you?"
   "I _____ ."
   "You know you shouldn't believe all those rumours."
   "Come on. There's usually some truth in them. They say old Smith got a promotion to Treasury Board."
   "I'll believe it when I see it."

je l'ai appris à travers les branches	*lo supe por ahí; me lo dijo un pajarito*	*got it from unofficial sources; heard a rumour*

6. "What's bugging Bill? He hasn't been himself lately."
   "I'm not sure but I think he's still mad about not getting that promotion last month."
   "Yeah. I think you've _____ . Just the other day I heard him complaining that good employees aren't appreciated around here."

tu as mis le doigt dessus; tu as visé juste	*diste en el clavo; lo atinaste*	*given exactly the right answer*

GOT IT STRAIGHT FROM THE HORSE'S MOUTH

13

7. "Have you heard there's going to be a big reorganization?"
"There are always rumours about a reorganization."
"This isn't just a rumour. I got it _____ ."

"You mean the Deputy Minister himself?"
"That's right."
"Well, I guess he should know."

de très bonne source   *lo supe de buena fuente*   *from the authoritative source*

8. "So you're getting the boss's job, eh!"
"No I'm not. Who told you that?"
"Nobody <u>told</u> me. But, when I see a guy measuring the boss's office and moving the furniture around the way you've been doing, I can _____ ."
"Look, please don't say anything. The official announcement won't be made until next week."
"Oh, I won't breathe a word. You can count on me."

c'est aussi clair que deux   *llegar a la conclusión*   *make a deduction*
et deux font quatre;   *from the evidence*
sauter aux conclusions

9. "Well, Brian, you must excuse me. I'm due at a meeting. But Bob here will show you around some more and introduce you to the rest of the staff."
"Thank you very much for spending so much time with me, Mr. Hudson."
"I'm leaving you in good hands. Bob has been with us for 15 years and, believe me, he really _____ ."

connaît les rouages   *conoce su trabajo*   *knows all aspects of the job;*
has a lot of knowledge
or experience of the subject

14

10. "Doug, have you seen item four on the agenda for tomorrow's meeting?"
    "You mean the proposal on a computerized information system?"
    "Right. That's the one."
    "Yeah. I've read it and I think we should do a cost analysis before we make a decision on it."
    "That's just what I was going to say. You _____ ."
    "Since we obviously see eye to eye on it, let's try to persuade the others to see things our way."

tu m'as sorti les mots de la bouche   *me quitaste la palabra de la boca*   *said exactly what I was going to say*

Answers on page 83.

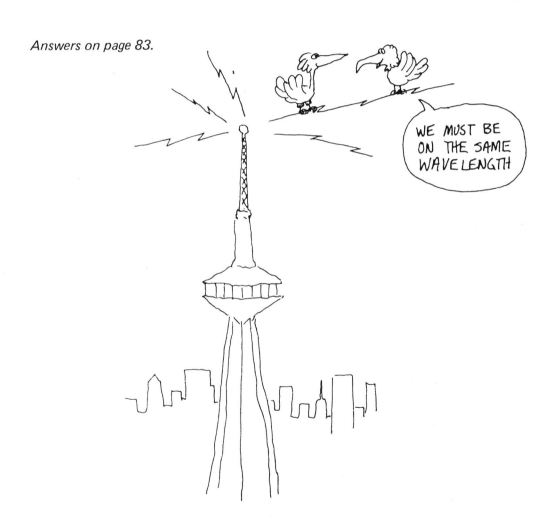

15

SECTION 4

Failure

a. was a flop
b. missed the boat
c. bit off more than he can chew
d. caught red-handed
e. got out of hand

f. on the blink
g. haven't got a leg to stand on
h. went to pieces
i. drew a blank
j. on the rocks

Fill in the blanks with the best idiom from the list above. Use the equivalents below each context in making your choice.

1. "When is Jerry expected back at work?"
   "Not for a long time. I went to see him on the weekend and he was in really bad shape."
   "Still, eh? I knew that when his wife and kids were killed he just _____ ."
   "Yeah, and since then, he's had one nervous breakdown after another."
   "Poor guy."

est tombé en morceaux;　　　　*quedó deshecho*　　　　*broke down;*
tout s'est écroulé　　　　　　　　　　　　　　　　　　　　*became crazy*

16

2. "Hi, Ron. How did your talk go at the conference?"
   "Horrible! I tried to explain our new approach to T-groups but it was over their heads.
   Most of them left before I finished. The whole thing _____ ."
   "It couldn't have been as bad as all that. I just got a request from a guy who was there,
   who wants you to give your talk at another conference."
   "Forget it!"

   a été un fiasco;   *fue un fracaso; fue un fiasco*   *was a total failure*
   a été un échec

3. "I tell you, Andy, I'm going to sue that guy."
   "Sue him for what?"
   "For wrecking my car."
   "Come on, Bill. You were following too close. It's the
   driver behind who is responsible, not the one in front. If
   you take him to court, you _____ .
   The law says you were in the wrong."

   tu n'as pas d'argument valable;   *no tienes*   *haven't got a valid argument*
   tu n'as aucune chance   *suficiente argumento*

4. (A couple returning to a real estate agent)
   "Hi, Joe. Hi, Edith. Still house-hunting?"
   "Yes, but not very sucessfully. I guess we really _____ when we
   didn't buy that bungalow in Orleans."
   "Yeah. That was a real bargain."
   "You wouldn't have another one like that, eh? "
   "I have one just like it — but it's $5,000 more."

   nous avons manqué le bâteau   *perdimos la oportunidad*   *missed our chance*

5. "Linda, would you give Rick a hand with the report on our staffing requirements for the next fiscal year?"

"I offered to help him but he insisted he could handle it on his own."

"Well, the Management Committee wants the report by Monday and Rick says he'll need help to have it ready on time."

"So, he admits he _____ . I told him so."

avait les yeux plus gros que la panse   *el que mucho abarca poco aprieta*   *accepted more than he could manage*

6. "Did you find that book I asked you to get for me?"
   "No, I'm afraid not. I tried the department library, the
   National Library and all the other libraries in town
   but I _____ . Then I
   called the bookstores but none of them ever heard of
   it."
   "Maybe I gave you the wrong title. Let me check."
   "<u>Now</u> you tell me!"

HE BIT OFF MORE
THAN HE COULD
CHEW.

je n'ai pas eu de succès;
ça n'a pas marché

no encontré nada

didn't get the desired results;
didn't have any success

7. "What do you mean, we ought to see a marriage counsellor?"
   "Let's face it, Brian. For the past two years all we've done is live in the same house. There's
   nothing left of our marriage."
   "Are you saying you want a divorce?"
   "No, I'm saying that our marriage is _____ and I think we need
   professional help."

en sérieuses difficultés   *tanbaleándose*   *wrecked;*
                                                                                  in difficulty

8. (A special news bulletin)
   "The police were called in last night during a demonstration on Parliament Hill. What started out as
   a peaceful march to protest the present high unemployment rate, soon _____
   _____ when demonstrators started throwing rocks and exchanging blows with the police.
   Ten people, including three policemen, were injured."

est devenu   *se armó la pelotera;*   *became uncontrollable*
incontrôlable   *and disorderly*
                                se armó la grande

19

9. "Hey, did you hear that Saunders got fired?"
   "No kidding! What happened?"
   "He was robbing the company."
   "Is there any chance they made a mistake?
   He seemed to be such an honest guy."
   "No way. The night guard caught him in the
   director's office, with the safe open, stuffing
   money and bonds into his attaché case."
   "In other words, he got _____
   _____."
   "I'll say."

   pris en flagrant délit;
   pris, la main dans le sac

   lo pillaron con las manos en la masa

   caught in the act

10. "Oh, no! "
    "What's the problem? "
    "The photocopy machine has broken down again."
    "Better send for the repairman."
    "Not again! That's the third time this week this machine's gone _____ ."
    "Maybe, we need a new photocopier."

    est en panne   *se descompone*   *out of order;*
                                                                         broken down

Answers on page 83.

SECTION 5

Success or Strong Interest

a. kill two birds with one stone
b. in the bag
c. snowballed
d. going over big
e. turns me on
f. calling the shots
g. made quite a name for herself
h. came out ahead
i. get a load of
j. got it made

Fill in the blanks with the best idiom from the list above. Use the equivalents below each context in making your choice.

1. "I sometimes wonder who's running this country."
   "What do you mean?"
   "Well, from what I see in the papers and on TV, it's the unions and big business that are _____
   _____ ."

   dirigent;   *están a cargo;*   *directing everything; in charge*
   mènent la barque   *llevan las riendas; dirigen*

2. (In a pub)

"I see you're drinking that new Danish beer."

"Yeah. It's great. It's got a special taste that's quite different from Canadian beer. A lot of people are switching to it."

"Yeah, it's _____ everywhere in Canada. Probably due to their big ad campaign."

"No, it's the taste. Try it. You'll like it."

connaît un grand succès;	*es un éxito;*	*a success;*
fait fureur	*ha hecho furor*	*receiving a lot of attention*

3. "Well, how much did you lose at the track last night?"

"I didn't lose anything. As a matter of fact I _____ ."

"Maybe you won last night but in the long run you always lose."

j'ai fini par gagner	*salí ganando;*	*won; ended in a*
	gané	*position of advantage*

KILLING TWO BIR

4. "So where is this great new stereo equipment, Eric?"
   "I've set it up in the basement . . . . Here it is. What do you think?"
   "Wow! Far out! That is beautiful equipment. _____ that
   amplifier and those speakers! Are they ever powerful! They must be at least a thousand watts."

   (re)garde-moi ça   *mira*   *look at(that)*

5. "That was a great game last night, eh? "
   "Sure was. I never thought the Yankees could win after being down 6-3 in the ninth inning."
   "Nobody did. Everybody was sure the game was _____ for the
   Red Sox."
   "They've been saying the whole series is a sure thing for the Red Sox, but after last night's game
   my money's on the Yankees."
   "O.K. How much do you want to bet? "

   partie gagnée;   *lo tenía en la mano;*   *a sure thing; a sure win*
   l'affaire était dans le sac   *lo tenía ganado*

TH ONE STONE

23

6. (A guest speaker is introduced)

"Until a few years ago there was little talk in Canada of the need for gun control. Outbreaks of violence in the recent past, however, raised the question of the need for stricter gun control and, in many parts of the country, small groups of concerned citizens got together to try to solicit support in their campaign to force the government to pass strict legislation against the carrying of firearms. The movement has _____ in recent months and a national action committee has now been formed. With us tonight we have the chairperson of that committee, Henrietta Perkins. Good evening, Ms Perkins . . . "

a fait boule de neige   *tomado fuerza*   *has increased greatly*

7. "Who's the new A.D.M.* going to be, do you know?"   *Assistant Deputy Minister*
   "Yes, it was announced this morning. It's Jennie Pinkerton."
   "That name rings a bell."
   "It should. She _____ in her last department. She joined the government as a middle manager 18 months ago and now she's a senior executive."
   "Wow. That's fast. She really must have what it takes."

s'est fait un nom;   *se ha hecho famosa*   *got a good reputation*
s'est fait une réputation

24

8. Don: "Where are you off to, Fred? Our poker game was just warming up."

   Fred: "Don't sweat it guys. I won't be long. I'm just going to pick up some more beer."

   Lou: "Hey, Fred. There's a great pizza place right next door to the beer store. Why don't you _____ and pick up a couple of pizzas."

faire d'une pierre deux coups   *matar 2 pájaros de un tiro;*   *do two things at the same time*
                                   matar 2 pájaros de una pedrada

9. (Later the same evening)

   Lou: "Do you mind if I turn on the T.V. Fred? There's a Raquel Welch movie on."

   Fred: "You can't play poker and watch a movie at the same time."

   Lou: "I don't want to watch the movie. I just want to see Raquel. I think she's fantastic. She really _____ ."

   Don: "Yeah. She does things for me, too."

   Fred: "Lookit you guys. You came here to play poker, right? So shut up and play."

m'excite;   *me encanta;*   *excites me;*
m'emballe   *me emociona*   *stimulates my interest*

YOU'VE REALLY MADE QUITE A NAME FOR YOURSELF

10. "Gee. I hope none of us get laid off in the cutbacks that have just been announced."
    "Well, even if we do, Fred, you won't suffer. You've _____ ."
    "What do you mean?"
    "Look at all the shares you've got in the telephone company and your night club's going great, too."

    tu as la vie belle;   *está todo de tu parte*   *nothing to worry about because*
    tu te la coules douce   *you are in a secure position*

    Answers on page 83.

TEST 1

Based on Sections 1-5

This is a test of some of the idiomatic expressions which you met in the first 5 sections.

Since this is a review, the contexts are shorter and there are only English equivalents given for each item.

The exact number of words required is indicated each time by the number of blanks.

You should be able to get at least 15 out of 20 correct the first time through. If you get fewer than 15 correct you should review the first 5 sections before going on to section 6.

The answers are on page 83.

1.
"How come this cassette won't play when I switch it on?"
"(It) _____ _____ . I don't know a thing about cassette players."

I don't understand it

2.
"You've been reading the newspaper for the last two hours, Robertson. It's _____ _____ you started doing some work."

long overdue (that)

3.
"Do the letters P.P.B.S. mean anything to you?"
"Yeah. That _____ _____ _____ . I think it stands for Program Planning and Budgeting Systems."

stirs a memory

4.
"Do you like the Rolling Stones' music?"
"I'll say! Any kind of rock music really _____ _____ _____ ."

excites me

5.
"How was Howard's presentation of the new long range planning proposal accepted by the Management Committee?"
"It _____ _____ _____ . They thought it was a great idea."

was a great success

BLAH... BLAH... BLAH... BLAH... BLAH...

I COULDN'T GET A WORD IN EDGEWISE!

8.
"Could you run off 10 copies of each of these documents for me, please?"
"I'm sorry. The machine's gone _____ _____ _____."
"Not again!"

out of order; broken down

9.
"Since you're going to pick up Nancy from hockey practice why don't you _____ _____ _____ _____ _____ _____ and pick up Billy after his ballet class?"

do two things at the same time

10.
"Did you explain your new idea to the boss over lunch?"
"No way. He talked so much I _____ _____ _____ _____ _____ _____."

didn't have a chance to say anything

11.
"How was the party last night?"
"It _____ _____ _____. Only six people showed up."
"They expected 40 people, so at least there must have been plenty to drink."

was a total failure

12.
"Did you remember to bring the book you promised me?"
"I'm sorry. It completely _____ _____ _____.
I'll bring it tomorrow."

escaped my memory

6.
"We'll have to put some controls on this flexible hours business. Everyone's arriving late and leaving early. It's a real mess."
"I agree. Things are _____ _____ _____ _____."

going out of control

7.
"Would you give me a hand with the annual report, please?"
"I offered to help you but you said you could do it on your own."
"Don't rub it in. I admit I _____ _____ _____ _____ _____ _____ _____."

accepted more than I can manage

13.
"Do you and your wife go to the movies much?"
"Only ____ ____ ____ ____ ____ . I think the last movie we saw was 'Last Tango in Paris' when it first came out."

rarely

14.
"Did it take you long to do the test on idiomatic expressions?"
"Are you kidding? It was easy. I finished it ____ ____ ____ ____ ."

in a very short time

15.
"Gentlemen, I realize that, in the short term, switching to a computerized system seems very expensive. However, ____ ____ ____ ____ it will save us millions."

in the end; over a long period

16.
"Who told you Janet's getting the Director's job?"
"I heard it ____ ____ ____ . I don't remember exactly who said it."

in informal office talk

BILL'S MARRIAGE IS REALLY ON THE ROCKS

17.

"Hey, Bill ____ ____ ____ ____ this new slide projector! Is it ever neat!"

"Yeah. That's really something."

take a look at

18.

"It's true about classes finishing early today!"

"Who told you?"

"I got it ____ ____ ____ ____ ____ ."

"You mean the school principal?"

"Yes."

the highest authority concerned

19.

"I've been studying the instructions for assembling your new model airplane, son, and I ____ ____ ____ ____ ____ ____ them."

"It's easy, Daddy. I'll show you."

don't understand them

20.

"I don't advise you to put in a grievance on this one, Jack. You ____ ____ ____ ____ ____ ____ ____ . The supervisor was within his rights."

don't have a valid argument

SECTION 6

Money Matters

a. in the red
b. sell like hot cakes
c. foot the bill
d. what a rip-off
e. flat broke
f. penny pincher
g. can't make ends meet
h. cost you an arm and a leg
i. corner the market
j. cut corners

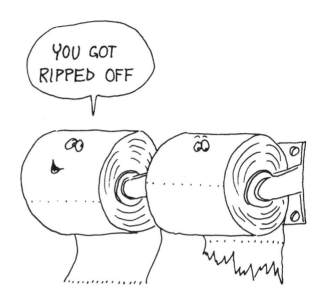

Fill in the blanks with the best idiom from the list above. Use the equivalents below each context in making your choice.

1. "Got your tickets for the Grey Cup yet?"
   "Not yet. There's still plenty of time."
   "Are you kidding? You'd better buy them today or you'll miss the boat. Those tickets always
   _____ ."
   "Come on. I know there's always a big demand for them but the game is still months away."

   se vendent comme des petits   se vende como pan caliente   sell quickly
   pains chauds

2. "How's your collection for the United Way going?"

   "Pretty good. Everybody has been very generous — except old MacDonald. He wouldn't give a cent. And you should have heard him!"

   "Sorry. I forgot to warn you about him. He never gives anything no matter how good the cause. He's a real _____ ."

   "Must be his Scotch blood."

   un grippe-sou   *tacaño; apretado*   *miserly person*

3. "Excuse me, there's a mistake on the bill. What's this 15% at the bottom?"

   "That's the service charge, sir."

   "What do you mean, service charge? The service was terrible. We had to wait 20 minutes before we even got the menus. The food was cold. The steak was tough and overcooked. The French fries were soggy. And now you want to charge an extra 15%. _____ !"

   ce sont des voleurs;   *es un robo;*   *it's robbery*
   c'est du vol   *es una estafa*

4. "Did you go house-hunting on the weekend again?"

   "Yeah, but I'm beginning to give up hope of ever finding a good house at the right price."

   "Did you go see the development I was telling you about?"

   "Sure. We went there on Sunday. I like the layout but the construction is pretty poor. The contractor obviously tried to _____ to reduce costs."

   prendre des raccourcis   *economizar*   *build in the cheapest way*

5. "I see World Business Machines has just bought out two more of their competitors. They are obviously out to _____ in office machines."

   "Yeah, they'll soon have a complete monopoly. It's high time the government did something about these giant corporations."

   (s')accaparer   *acaparar el mercado*   *establish*
   le marché   *a monopoly*

6. "Say, Bob. Could you lend me ten bucks until payday?"
   "Sorry, Gerry. I'm afraid I'm _____ . In fact, if I didn't have a bus ticket I wouldn't be able to get home tonight."

   fauché; sans le sou   *sin un centavo*   *without any money*

7. "So, to sum up, gentlemen, there simply isn't enough demand for our product. We've been operating _____ for the last year, and the only way to get into the black is to lay off some of the workers."

   déficitaire; dans le rouge   *sin fondos*   *in an unprofitable way; at a loss*

8. "Gee, Rick, I didn't know you were a bartender. When did you leave the government?"
   "I haven't left. I'm still with the same department."
   "So you're moonlighting, eh?"
   "Yeah. I couldn't support my family and keep up the mortgage payments on my government salary alone."
   "I know what you mean. I _____ these days, either. Do they need any more bartenders here?"

   je n'arrive pas à joindre   *a mí tampoco me alcanza;*   *can't earn what it*
   les deux bouts   *a mí tampoco me llega;*   *costs to live*
                                      no gano para vivir

9. "Where are you taking your wife tonight to celebrate your wedding anniversary?"
"We're going to Luigi's."
"Don't go there. It's way too expensive. It'll _____ ."
"I suppose so but their food is excellent."
"Listen. I know a new French restaurant where the cuisine is just as good, if not better, for about half the price."
"Oh really. Where is it?"

ça te coutera les yeux de la tête	*cuesta un ojo de la cara*	*cost you a fortune; cost you more than it is worth*

10. "O.K. you guys. You each owe me nine bucks. Pay up!"
"What for?"
"The drinks last night. You all drank plenty but you took off and made me _____ _____ on my own."
"I thought you said the drinks were on you."
"I meant the first round, not the whole night, damn it!"

payer la note	*pagar la cuenta*	*pay the bill*

WE CAN'T MAKE ENDS MEET...

Answers on page 85.

SECTION 7

Extremes or Excess

LAYING IT
ON THICK

a. the last straw
b. I've had it with
c. that takes the cake
d. we're splitting hairs
e. the tail wagging the dog
f. making a mountain out of a molehill
g. to add insult to injury
h. laying it on thick
i. pretty farfetched
j. got carried away

Fill in the blanks with the best idiom from the list above.
Use the equivalents below each context in making your choice.

1. "That damn technician completely screwed up my presentation."
   "Oh no! What happened? "
   "He told me he'd checked out all the equipment. I switched on the tape recorder, but it's only got one speed — the wrong speed. Then I went to the flip chart; the minute I touched it, one of the legs broke."
   "Oh no! That presentation was really important for us."
   "I didn't give up. I smiled at everybody and switched on the movie projector; the clown had put

the film in backwards. That was (1) _____ . I couldn't take any
more. I gave them a coffee break so I could fix things up."
"I hate to say 'I told you so' but I did say you were (2) _____
with all that a/v equipment."
"I know! You told me I was overdoing it with all that equipment."

(1) *ça a été la goutte d'eau*   (1) *el colmo*   (1) *the final problem in a*
    (qui a fait déborder le verre)   *series of problems*

(2) *tu exagérais*   (2) *exagerando*   (2) *carrying something to*
                                                                           extreme or excess

2. "Look here, everyone, this discussion seems to be getting out of hand. As chairperson of this
committee I think it's about time I intervened. As I see it we are all agreed on the general
principles, and what we're now discussing are minor details. I think _____
on this issue."
"You're right. Let's send out the policy directive as it now stands and let local managers work out
the details on how it should apply to their area."
"Hear! Hear!"

on coupe les cheveux   *buscarle cinco patas al gato*   *arguing about small,*
en quatre   *unimportant differences*

3. "It's a crisis — an absolute crisis."
"Come on now, Mike. The situation isn't that serious. It's a relatively minor problem, and we can
deal with it before it gets out of hand."
"It's a crisis, I tell you."
"Lookit. I think you're getting things all out of proportion. You're _____ .
Maybe you should take a couple of days rest."

tu fais une montagne   *estás haciendo una*   *thinking a small problem*
d'un grain de sable   *montaña de un grano*   *is a big one*
                                          de arena

4. "What are you looking so mad about?"

"It's Mike again. Every time there's a little problem he gets it all out of proportion."

"I know what you mean."

"I'm sick of him running into my office and telling me we've got a crisis on our hands. I tell you _____ him. If he tries to tell me one more time there's a crisis on, I'll kill him."

j'en ai assez de lui   *ya me colmó la paciencia;*   *I have come to the end*
           no lo aguanto más   *of my patience*

5. "I'm fed up with our so-called service units telling us operations managers how we should be doing things."

" 'So-called' services is right. They're supposed to give us the back-up services we ask them for. Instead of that they keep telling us to change our system to suit them."

"Things are completely turned around. It's a case of _____ ."

c'est le monde à l'envers   *haciendo las cosas al revés*   *the normal situation is reversed*

6. "What are you shaking your head about? "
   "I've just finished reading Steve's list of ways of motivating employees to work more efficiently.
   I really don't think many of his ideas are reasonable or practical. Most of them are _____
   _____ ."

   un peu trop poussées;   *un poco exageradas*   *rather exaggerated;*
   un peu trop fantaisistes   *out of touch with reality*

7. "Say, Steve, about that list of suggestions you gave me on ways of motivating employees . . . "
   "What did you think of it?"
   "Well, I really liked some of your ideas, but I'm afraid I found the others rather impractical and
   extreme."
   "I guess I _____ on some of them. I've probably been reading too
   much futurology, lately."

   je me suis laissé emporter   *me dejé llevar*   *lost my judgement because of*
   excitement

8. "I've had it with the hydro company."

"What have they done now?"

"Well, you know the electricity's been off since Sunday, we've had at least twenty blackouts in the last three months, some of them three days long, and now, (1) _____ _____ , we just got a bill for over $500.00."

"You mean they have the nerve to send out bills at a time like this. That's incredible; (2) _____ . We should send them a bill for all the frozen meat and other food we've had to throw out."

(1) ajouter l'insulte à l'injure

(2) ça gagne le premier prix; il ne manquait plus que ça

(1) para colmo

(2) eso fue lo último

(1) to make things worse

(2) that's the limit

Answers on page 85.

THE TAIL
WAGGING
THE DOG

SECTION 8

Compromise or Balance

a. make allowances for

b. meet them halfway

c. give him a break

d. take what he says with a grain of salt

e. sits on the fence

f. find a happy medium

g. let sleeping dogs lie

h. bend over backwards

i. heads or tails

j. sleep on it

Fill in the blanks with the best idiom from the list above. Use the equivalents below each context in making your choice.

1. "As to which of our two official languages we should use for the Task Force work, I don't think we should argue about this issue any more. I'm sure we can _____ by allowing each person to use the language of his choice. That way everyone should be satisfied."

trouver un juste milieu   *llegar a un acuerdo;*   *find a compromise*
                                        encontrar el justo medio

40

2. "That new guy in the stockroom is so slow it's unbelievable. I just spent half an hour waiting for him to find me a box of notepads."
    "Come on, Phil. You have to _____ the fact that he's only been here a week and it's a pretty big stockroom."

    tenir compte   *tomar en cuenta*   *judge the situation*
    du fait que   *by the circumstances*

3. (Three months later)
    "So help me, I'm going to fire that stock clerk. He's been here for months now, but his speed hasn't improved at all. I've warned him enough. This time I've had it with him. He's out."
    "Aw, come on, Phil. _____ . He deserves another chance. He's trying."

    donne-lui une chance   *dále una oportunidad;*   *offer him another chance*
                               dále chance

4. "But you don't know my parents. They've got such old fashioned ideas. They want me to be home by 11 o'clock on Saturday nights."
    "That seems a little strict but, you know, if you want them to give you more freedom, you've got to be willing to _____ sometimes. You can't expect to get your own way in everything."

    faire la moitié   *tienes que dar*   *give up part of what*
    du chemin   *tu brazo a torcer*   *you want to reach*
                                                         agreement

5. "Was Anderson serious when he said the company's going to lay off a couple of hundred men?"
    "Oh, he's always spreading rumours. Sometimes there's a little truth in what he says but, in general, you should _____ ."

    prendre ce qu'il dit   *creerle la mitad*   *not believe*
    avec un grain de sel   *de lo que dice*   *all he says*

6. "How do you like having old slowpoke McKay for a boss?"
"Look. He may be old and slow but he really looks out for his staff. He'll _____
_____ to help any one of us out."
"Good for him. It's pretty rare to find a boss who'll do all he possibly can for his staff. Usually all they care about is their next promotion."

se fendra en quatre

hace todo lo posible;
se mata

make a
great effort

GIVE US
A BREAK

7. "Donaldson really bugs me when there's a problem around here. He never supports one side or the other."
"Right. I've noticed he always _____ no matter what's being discussed."
"It's high time he learned that the only thing he's likely to get from that position is a sore rear."

ne veut pas se compromettre;
ne veut pas se mouiller les pieds

está siempre
indeciso

does not want to choose
or decide

42

8. "Gee. I'm really flattered by your offering me a promotion, but I'm not sure how I feel about moving to Vancouver."

   "I realize it's a big decision to make, Bert. I don't expect you to give me an answer immediately. Why don't you go home and _____ . Let me know your decision tomorrow or the day after if you need more time."

prend le temps qu'il faut pour y réfléchir; *la nuit porte conseil*	*lo piensas bien;* *lo consultas con tu almohada*	*think about it for awhile*

9. "Is Sally in?"

   "I hope you're not going to bother her with the Gordon affair again."

   "So what if I do?"

   "Why don't you _____ ? Bothering her about that again isn't going to change a damn thing. The decision on it was final."

   "Mind your own business."

   pourquoi déterrer les morts

   lo dejas tal cual

   avoid making more trouble on the same issue

HA HA HA HA HA·HA HA

A HAPPY MEDIUM

BENDING OVER BACKWARDS

10. "It's your turn to pay, eh?"
    "No way. I got the last round."
    "No you didn't. I remember giving the waitress a twenty dollar bill."
    "That was two rounds ago."
    "Lookit. There's a quick way to settle this before we die of thirst. I've got a quarter here. You call
    it. _____ ?"

pile ou face

cara o sello;
aguila o sol (México)

(Expression used when
tossing a coin)

Answers on page 85.

SECTION 9

Complaining or Commiserating

a. pull the wool over other people's eyes
b. a stab in the back
c. pay lip service to
d. goofs off
e. get away with murder
f. that's hitting below the belt
g. talk behind his back
h. taking her for granted
i. get the runaround
j. isn't pulling his (own) weight

Fill in the blanks with the best idiom from the list above.
Use the equivalents below each context in making your choice.

1. "I know what I'd do to those kids next door if they were mine."
   "I agree. They're getting completely out of hand."
   "It's high time their parents started disciplining them instead of letting them _____."
   "Young parents are all the same these days. They're far too permissive."

   s'en tirer impunément   *salirse con la suya;*   *do bad things without*
                                    hacer lo que quieran   *being punished*

2. "I can't stand Linda Brown. She's really two-faced."
   "In what way?"
   "Well, the boss thinks she's a great worker because, whenever he's around, she really tries to impress him. But when he's not there she doesn't do any work at all. Instead, she
   (1) _____ all the time."
   "I hate people like that who try to (2) _____ . Never mind, one of these days he's going to find out the truth."

   (1) badine; niaise   *(1) no hace nada*   *(1) is lazy and fools around*
   (2) jettent de la poudre   *(2) engañarle a alguien*   *(2) deceive someone into*
   aux yeux de quelqu'un   *thinking well of them*

3. "I don't think he's the right man for the job. You know, he's left his wife and he's living with another woman."
   "Come on. We're here to judge the candidates on their merit. His private life is none of our business."
   "You're right. I'm sorry. It wasn't fair of me to bring up his private life. _____.
   Let's consider his abilities and aptitudes."

   c'est un coup bas   *es un golpe bajo; no es derecho*   *that goes against one's sense of justice and sportsmanship*

46

4. "How are things going on the selection board, Sue?"
   "Don't talk to me about that board. I've had it with them."
   "How come?"
   "Well, they talk about the merit principle a lot, but when it comes to making a decision on a candidate, it's a different story. They bring in all kinds of factors that have nothing to do with merit."
   "I agree with you. It's not enough to _____ a principle. You've got to do something about it."

   lancer des paroles en l'air   *decir algo sin creerlo*   *show support by words only and not by actions*

5. "It's about time somebody told Jack that every member of a team has to do his share of the work."
   "Yeah, I've noticed he (1) _____ on our team."
   "Of course, it's our own fault. We should tell him right to his face that he isn't doing enough."
   "You're right. Instead of telling him to his face, all we've done is (2) _____ ."

   (1) il ne fait pas sa part

   (2) lui parler dans le dos

   (1) no cumple con la parte que le corresponde; no hace lo que le toca

   (2) hablar a sus espaldas

   (1) doesn't do his fair share of the work

   (2) discuss him when he isn't there

47

6. "No wonder people complain about poor service when they phone a government department. I've just spent half an hour trying to get an answer to a very simple question."

"I bet the first person told you to call another number, and then they told you to call a third number, and at the third number . . . "

"Exactly, Now I know what people mean when they say they _____ when they phone the government."

font courir d'un côté et de l'autre;
renvoient quelqu'un de Caïphe à Pilate

me mandan de aquí para allá;

me mandan de un lugar a otro

are constantly told that the place they have called or gone to is not the right one

7. "Gee, do I ever miss Rachel. This new secretary doesn't seem to know which end is up half the time."

"Right. I've noticed that."

"I'm really sorry now I didn't tell Rachel what a good job she was doing."

"I guess we all made the mistake of _____ _____. Maybe she wouldn't have left

if we'd told her how much we appreciated her."

ne pas lui dire combien on appréciait son aide

no apreciar su trabajo

receiving the benefit of her good work without praising or thanking her

MPHFF!!

HITTING BELOW THE BELT

8. "How's Colin feeling about losing the nomination at the meeting last night?"

   "Pretty bad, I'm afraid, and I don't blame him. At least thirty people promised to vote for him but didn't in the end. And they were people he trusted completely."

   "Yeah. When they voted for the other guy it was _____ for Colin."

   "That's politics, I guess."

un coup dans le dos	una puñalada por la espalda; una mala jugada	an act that hurt a friend or a trusting person

Answers on page 85.

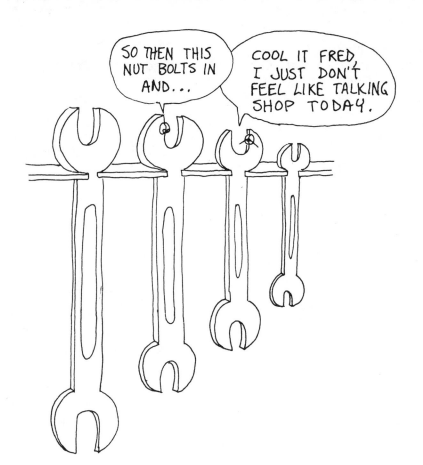

SECTION 10

Socializing

a. thanks all the same
b. I don't feel up to
c. talking shop
d. feeling under the weather
e. have a night out on the town
f. put my foot in it
g. giving a housewarming party
h. isn't it a small world
i. can I take a rain check
j. speak of the devil

Fill in the blanks with the best idiom from the list above.
Use the equivalents below each context in making your choice.

1. "Good night, Dick. It was a great party. Thanks for inviting us."
   "I hope you two aren't leaving already. It's still early."
   "I think I'd better get Tom home to bed. He's _____ . He's had a
   touch of the flu lately and your punch is pretty potent stuff. I guess Tom underestimated it."

   il n'est pas en forme;   *no se siente bien*   *slightly ill*
   il ne se sent pas bien

2. Mike to Barb: " . . . and as for Andy, he's always goofing off. He spends his time in the typing pool hustling the girls and . . .".

   Andy arrives: "Girls! You've said the magic word, Mike."

   Mike: "Oh, hi Andy. _____ . I was just telling Barb, here, about you."

   Andy: "Nice things, I hope."

   Mike: "Sure, Andy."

parlant de la bête
(on en voit la tête)

hablando del rey
de Roma

(Expression used when the person you have just been talking about arrives.)

3. (A few minutes later)

   "What are you looking so guilty about?"

   "You know me and my big mouth. I just _____ again."

   "Who did you insult this time?"

   "Well, I was talking to that tall girl over there — Barb — and telling her about the guys at the office and . . . uh . . . well nobody told me she was Andy's fiancée . . ."

   "Aw Mike! I can't take you any̲where!"

je me suis mis les pieds dans
les plats;

j'ai fait une gaffe

metí la pata

made a social mistake;
committed a social gaffe

FEELING UNDER THE WEATHER

4. "Get out your new dress. We're going to _____."
"What are we celebrating?"
"I've just been given a promotion."
"Hey great! Now that's worth celebrating. Give me ten minutes and I'll be ready to go."

sortir pour fêter; *faire la foire*	*celebrar;* *ir de juerga;* *salir de parranda*	*go out to celebrate;* *have an evening's celebration* *away from home*

5. "Where are you off to, John?"
   "St. Laurent Shopping Centre."
   "Jump in. We'll give you a ride. It's on our way home."
   "That's O.K. My wife's picking me up in a couple of minutes. _____ ."

   merci tout de même;   *gracias de todos modos*   *(Polite expression used*
   merci quand même   *when you completely refuse*
                                                                      an invitation or offer.)

6. "Come on, you guys. This is a party, not the staff room. You've been sitting here talking about
      work for the last hour. Come on and join the party."
   "O.K. We're coming."
   "But you have to promise you'll stop _____ ."

   parler du bureau;   *hablar del trabajo*   *speaking about your work*
   parler du travail

7. "Hi, Lucy. How's the new house? Are you all unpacked yet?"
   "Are you kidding? It's going to take us months to unpack all those boxes."
   "Aw well, you'll get a lot of it done on the long weekend."
   "I doubt it. We're _____ on Friday. Are you and Eric free that
      evening? If you don't mind drinking out of plastic cups, maybe you'd like to come?"

   on pend la crémaillère   *dar una fiesta para*   *giving a party to celebrate*
                                      inaugurar la casa   *moving into our new house*

8. "Excuse me. The restaurant seems to be full. Do you mind if we share this table?"
   "No. Have a seat . . . For heaven's sake! Pete Fraser! Fancy meeting you here in Nassau."
   "Frank Harris! I thought you'd be slaving away back at the hospital."
   "Me too! I didn't know you were planning a vacation. Imagine us ending up in the same place."
   " _____ ?"

   que le monde est petit   *qué pequeño es el mundo;*   *(Expression used when you meet*
                                      el mundo es un pañuelo   *someone you know whom you did*
                                                                    not expect to see there.)

9. (Telephone conversation)

"Hello."

"Hello, Heather. It's Bert here. There's a really good movie on at the Odeon and I thought maybe you'd like to go."

"Oh, I'd really like to, Bert, but I'm afraid (1) _____ going out tonight. I had a pretty rough day at the library and I'm absolutely pooped. (2) _____ ?"

"Sure. How about tomorrow night?"

"That sounds great."

(1) *je ne suis pas en forme;*
    je me sens pas de taille

(2) *une autre fois, peut-être;*
    c'est partie remise

(1) *no tengo ganas;*
    no siento deseos de ir

(2) *dejémoslo para la*
    próxima

(1) *I don't have the strength to*

(2) *(Expression used to*
    postpone the acceptance of
    an invitation.)

Answers on page 85.

54

TEST 2

Based on Sections 6-10

This is a test of some of the idiomatic expressions which you met in sections 6-10.

Since this is a review, the contexts are shorter and there are only English equivalents given for each item.

The exact number of words required is indicated each time by the number of blanks.

You should be able to get at least 15 out of 20 correct the first time through. If you get fewer than 15 correct you should review sections 6-10 before going on to section 11.

The answers are on page 85.

1.
"I've got to find a job that pays more than the one I've got now. We're up to our ears in debt and we ____ ____ ____ ____."

can't earn what it costs to live

2.
"It isn't a crisis at all. It's only a minor problem. You're ____ ____ ____ ____ ____ ____ ____."

thinking a small problem is a big one

3.
"Don't believe everything Shirley tells you. You should ____ what she says ____ ____ ____ ____."

not believe all she says

ALRIGHT YOU GUYS! QUIT TRYING TO PULL THE WOOL OVER MY EYES AND GET BACK TO WORK!

BOSS

A PENNY PINCHER

OUCH!

4.
"I typed that report five times because Mr. Robertson kept making changes to it. But then, when he asked me to do it again with double spacing instead of single spacing that ＿＿ ＿＿ ＿＿ ＿＿. I told him he could type it himself."

the final problem in a series of problems

5.
"Lookit. We agreed to have a night out on the town to enjoy ourselves not to talk about work. Let's stop ＿＿ ＿＿."

discussing work

6.
"It's high time someone told Gordon that each member of a team has to do his fair share of work."
"Yeah, I've noticed he isn't ＿＿ ＿＿ (＿＿) ＿＿ on our team."

doing his share of the work

7.
"You'd better hurry up and buy your tickets for the Gilles Vigneault concert. They're ＿＿ ＿＿ ＿＿ ＿＿."

selling quickly

8.
"It's not enough to ＿＿ ＿＿ ＿＿ ＿＿ a principle. You have to prove you believe it by your actions."

show support by words only and not be actions

9.
"I'd love to come and see your new apartment but I'm afraid I'm busy tonight. ＿＿ ＿＿ ＿＿ ＿＿ ＿＿ ＿＿?"
"Sure. How about tomorrow night?"
"Tomorrow's fine."

can I postpone the invitation

10.
"You mean to say he charged you twenty dollars for a five dollar ticket to the game. ＿＿ ＿＿ ＿＿!"

that's robbery

11.
"Muriel never gives a definite opinion on one side or the other of any issue. She always ＿＿ ＿＿ ＿＿ ＿＿."

does not want to choose or decide

56

12.

"Claude will do everything possible for his staff. He'll ____ ____ ____ to help any one of them."

make a great effort

13.

"The receptionist sent me to Room 320 but there they told me to go to Room 875 and then I was told to go to 1215."

"You really ____ ____ ____ , eh?"

sent to many different places

14.

"What a surprise meeting our next door neighbours while we were camping out West."

"Yes. ____ ____ ____ ____ ____ ?"

(Expression used when you meet a friend in a place where you did not expect to see him.)

15.

"That John Richards is really deceitful. He doesn't do any work but he's fooled the boss into thinking he's a great worker."

"I can't stand people like that who ____ ____ ____ ____ ____ ____ ____ ."

deceive others into thinking well of them

16.

"This house is really poorly constructed. The builder obviously tried to ____ ____ to reduce costs."

build in the cheapest way

17.

"Very few of Steve's ideas are reasonable or practical. Most of them are pretty ____ ."

out of touch with reality, exaggerated

18.
"I don't think we should argue about these minor details. I think we're ____ ____ ."

arguing about small, unimportant details

19.
"Me and my big mouth. I really ____ ____ ____ ____ ____ today. I was telling everybody in the office how badly the boss treated his secretary and then, when I turned around, he was standing there, looking furious."

committed a gaffe

20.
"Since you two obviously don't see eye to eye on this issue let's try to ____ ____ ____ ____ that you can agree on."

find a compromise

SECTION 11

Giving or Seeking Information

a. read between the lines
b. keep me posted
c. off the top of my head
d. asked him point blank
e. speak off the cuff
f. give me a rundown
g. off the record
h. spilled the beans
i. drop you a line
j. don't beat around the bush

Fill in the blanks with the best idiom from the list above.
Use the equivalents below each context in making your choice.

1. "Bad news, Stephen. Our after-dinner speaker just called to say he can't come because the airport is snowed in. You'll have to fill in for him."
   "Please find somebody else. You know I'm no good at making speeches even when I have time to prepare them. I'm even worse when I have to _____ ."

   parler de façon impromptue;   *improvisar*   *give a talk extemporaneously,*
   parler à l'improviste   *without preparation*

2. "Say, Bob, what was the Director's answer when you asked him if the rumours about lay-offs were true?"
   "He was pretty vague, I'm afraid."
   "Maybe your question wasn't direct enough."
   "It couldn't have been more direct. I _____ if any employees would be laid off in the next few months."

   j'ai demandé carrément;   *le pregunté directamente*   *asked specifically*
   j'ai demandé à brûle-pourpoint

OFF THE CUFF

3. (A week later)
   "O.K. Bob. We know you were called up to the Directors' meeting this morning. What did they say about lay-offs?"
   "Well . . . uh . . . you see . . . uh . . . it seems that for the time being, at least and . . . uh . . . if the marketing report confirms the . . . uh . . . estimated trend and . . . uh . . . provided . . ."
   "Come on Bob, Get to the point. _____ . We want a straight answer to the question. Are there going to be lay-offs or not?"

   ne tournez pas autour du pot   *no te vayas por las ramas;*   *don't avoid the question*
                                no le des vueltas al asunto

4. "Things seem to be going quite well in our Caribbean offices. Did you read their latest reports?"
   "Yes, I did. On the surface, things seem to be going well but if you _____
   I think you'll find there are some problems."
   "Really? I guess I'd better read those reports more carefully."

   lisez entre les lignes   *lees entre líneas*   *guess what is left unsaid*

5. "Good luck on your trip to the Maritimes, Helen."

"Thanks, Frank. I'll have a full report for you when I get back next month."

"I know we'll have a complete report in a month but I'd like to get some feedback before then, so _____ , eh?"

"Don't worry. I'll give you a call a couple of times a week and let you know how things are going."

tiens-moi au courant   manténme al día;   make sure I am informed
                                      manténme al corriente

6. "Gee, we're really going to miss you two, after all these years having you as neighbours. Now you're going to be five hundred miles away."

"Don't worry. We'll send you all the news. As soon as we're settled, I'll _____ and let you know how things are going."

je vous écrirai un mot   te escribiré   write you a letter

STOP BEATING AROUND THE BUSH!

7. "That seems to take care of the business on the agenda. But before we adjourn, I'd like each one of you to (1) _____ on your major projects. Let's start with you, Shirley. How long will it take before the new computerized system completely replaces the manual one?"

"I'm afraid I didn't bring the reports with me and I don't remember the exact dates for the completion of the various phases . . ."

"I just want a guesstimate."

"Well, (2) _____ , I'd say the new system will be in place within three months. I'll check on the details and give you a call this afternoon."

| (1) me donner un aperçu | (1) hacerme un resumen | (1) give me a summary |
| (2) de mémoire | (2) de lo que me acuerdo | (2) from memory; I guess |

8. "Hey, you promised you wouldn't tell the boss we took Friday afternoon off."
"Don't blame me. I didn't tell him. It was Ernie who _____ ."
"But he was with us."
"I guess he felt guilty and decided to confess."

| a vendu la mèche | ____se le salió | told the secret to a person who is not supposed to know |

KEEPING HIM POSTED

9. "Come on, John. We're old friends. I promise I won't print it until it's announced officially."
"O.K., but it's strictly _____ . If any of it gets into the newspapers before the Minister announces it officially, my head will roll."

| à ne pas répéter; à ne pas publier | confidencial | confidential; not to be published |

Answers on page 87.

SECTION 12

Things Going Wrong

A STUMBLING BLOCK

a. stumbling block
b. have to start from scratch
c. in a rut
d. can't get the hang of it
e. in a bind

f. going around in circles
g. inside out
h. upside down
i. is in for
j. scraping the bottom of the barrel

Fill in the blanks with the best idiom from the list above.
Use the equivalents below each context in making your choice.

1. "You must have gotten dressed in a hurry this morning."
   "What makes you say that?"
   "You've got your sweater on _____ ."
   "How can you tell?"
   "Well, I don't think the label is supposed to be on the outside."

   à l'envers   *al revés*   *so that the inside*
                                                                 is turned outside

2. "What made you decide to apply for that job in Belgium?"
   "Well you know, I've been working for the same company for ten years now. I like my work

63

but I feel like I'm _____ in this job. It just isn't as interesting
or challenging as it used to be."
"In that case a change will probably do you good."

ça devient routinier;   *se está haciendo una rutina*   *in a dull routine*
je me sens dans une ornière

JOE'S IN A RUT.

3. "Am I ever glad to see you."
   "What's up?"
   "It's this new film projector. I've been trying to thread a film for the last twenty minutes but I
   just _____ . I could put a film on the old projector in no time
   flat, but this one's got me beat."
   "Let me have a try."

   je n'ai pas le tour   *no sé como hacerlo funcionar;*   *don't know how to*
                                  no le encuentro la maña   *make it work*

4. "How are the negotiations for the new collective agreement going?"
   "They've broken down completely. The union side is taking it to conciliation."
   "That's a surprise. The last I heard everything was going well. What was it you couldn't reach
   agreement on?"
   "The _____ was the four-day work week."

   pierre d'achoppement   *el punto problemático*   *problem point;*
                                                                    difficulty

I CAN'T SEEM TO GET THE HANG OF IT!

5. "What's in the crate?"
   "I don't know. I can't get it open."
   "I'm not surprised. You're trying to open the bottom. Turn it over. It's easier to open from the top."
   "It was pretty stupid of me not to realize it was _____ .
   No wonder I was having so much trouble."

   sens dessus dessous   *de cabeza; al revés*   *the wrong way up*

6. "When's Phil due back from his vacation?"
   "Not for another couple of weeks. Why do you ask?"
   "I'm afraid he _____ an unpleasant surprise. They've reorganized his section out of existence."

   va certainement avoir;   *se va a encontrar*   *is unable to avoid;*
   peut s'attendre à   *will certainly get*

7. "Say, Yvonne, when does the typists' eligibility list expire?"
   "Next week, but we can extend it if you like."
   "Forget the extension. We'll run another competition. I've had too many complaints from supervisors about the last typists we hired from that list. It looks like we're _____ ."
   "Well, that's not surprising. We're getting to the bottom of the list and the remaining candidates just meet the minimum qualifications."

   on gratte le fond du pot   *haciendo uso del último recurso;*   *taking what is left after*
                                        llegando al fondo   *the best has been taken*

65

8. "Say, Gerry, I'm _____ . I've just been called to an urgent meeting at City Hall and I don't know how long it will take."
"What's your problem?"
"Well, you see, I've got really important clients coming, and I don't want to cancel or they might go to another company."
"Don't worry. If you're not back I'll take care of them for you. Just give me their files."

dans un dilemme;   *en un dilema;*   *in a dilemma;*
dans une mauvaise passe   *en una situación difícil*   *in a difficult situation*

9. "Look, it's been a long day and we're all tired. I don't think we're going to solve all these problems today."
"Wait a minute. I think we came up with some pretty good ideas."
"That was a couple of hours ago. Since then we've been repeating the same things. We're _____ _____ . Let's adjourn until tomorrow. Our minds will be clearer in the morning."

on tourne en rond   *dándole vueltas*   *talking without*
     al asunto   *any progress*

10. "I don't know how to tell you this but . . . uh . . . you know that pile of handwritten notes that were on your desk in the study . . . uh . . . well . . . I'm afraid the dog chewed them up."
"Oh, my God. That was the only copy of my term paper. I'll _____ again."
"I'm sorry. I tried smoothing out the few scraps that were left but the ink had run. It's totally illegible."

SCRAPING THE BOTTOM
OF THE BARREL...

je dois recommencer à zéro

tengo que volver a comenzar desde el principio

have to begin from nothing

Answers on page 87.

SECTION 13

Contradicting or Disagreeing

a. beside the point
b. barking up the wrong tree
c. have a bone to pick with you
d. so what?
e. doesn't hold water
f. take exception to
g. come off it
h. is at odds with
i. putting the cart before the horse
j. that's all very well and good but

Fill in the blanks with the best idiom from the list above.
Use the equivalents below each context in making your choice.

1. "Hold on a minute. There's no point discussing how we're going to give the course before we establish the course objectives."
   "You're right. We're _____ . Let's set the objectives first and then we can discuss how to attain them."

   on met la charrue   *haciendo las cosas*   *getting things in*
   devant les boeufs   *al revés*   *the wrong order*

2. "Hi, Roger. How are things?"

"Sally Langton — my favourite personnel officer. Just the person I wanted to see.
I _____ ."

"Oh-oh! What have I done now?"

"You promised to find me a temporary typist two days ago and I'm still waiting."

j'ai un petit compte *à régler avec toi*	*tengo una cuenta* *pendiente contigo;*	*have something to* *reproach you about*
	tengo un asunto que *arreglar contigo*	

3. ". . . so, in light of the two points I've just made, I'm sure you'll agree that your decision should be changed."

"(1) _____ , Max! You're getting carried away with your own rhetoric. Your arguments aren't convincing or valid."

"What's wrong with them?"

"Your first one is (2) _____ . It's totally irrelevant. And as for your second point, the theory you're basing it on is full of holes — your argument simply
(3) _____ ."

"Wait a minute, Anne, I (4) _____ your remark that my theory is full of holes. In fact, I got it out of *Psychology Tomorrow*."

(1) reviens-en; *arrête de dire des bêtises*	*(1) deja de decir tonterías*	*(1) don't talk nonsense;* *stop being silly*
(2) n'a aucun rapport *avec le sujet;* *ce n'est pas dans le sujet*	*(2) no tiene nada que ver*	*(2) is not on the subject*
(3) ne tient pas debout	*(3) no tiene base*	*(3) is faulty*
(4) je m'inscris en faux à	*(4) no admito*	*(4) find fault with;* *disagree with*

4. "If you guys think that presenting your petition to the board will get action you're
_____ ."
   "What makes you say that?"
   "Because it's the Mayor who makes all the decisions in this area."

   vous vous trompez royalement   *están equivocados;*   *choosing the wrong*
                                           están en un error   *course of action;*
                                                                          making a mistake

5. "Tell me, Mrs. Stevens, what made you decide to withdraw your child from his previous kinder-
   garten and bring him here?"
   "Well, basically because I find that their whole approach _____
   my own views on how a child should be raised and educated."

   ne concorde pas avec   *no concuerda con;*   *is in conflict with;*
                                   está en desacuerdo con   *is in disagreement with*

69

6. "Say, Doug, the chairman wants the financial reports for the first quarter."
   "Well, he can't have them until we find out which set of figures is correct. We're working on it night and day and I'd say that we'll have the problem licked in a couple of weeks."
   "_____ it won't satisfy the chairman. He wants those figures today."
   "Then he can have both sets."

tout cela est b(i)en beau mais	*todo eso está muy bien, pero; está muy bien, sin embargo*	*that's fine but; that's no good*

7. "Hey, did you hear the news? They've announced a cabinet shuffle. Our department has a new Minister."
   "_____ ? Why should I care? At our level it doesn't make any difference who the Minister is."
   "What an attitude!"

et après; puis après	*y qué*	*(Impolite reply showing that the speaker is not impressed by what has been said.)*

Answers on page 87.

SECTION 14

The Bureaucracy

a. don't rock the boat
b. up in the air
c. cut through the red tape
d. pass the buck
e. pulled strings
f. blew the whistle on
g. snowed under
h. pushed the panic button
i. gave him the axe
j. go over her head

Fill in the blanks with the best idiom from the list above.
Use the equivalents below each context in making your choice.

1. "I'm going to ask for a transfer to another section."
   "What's the problem?"
   "It's the supervisor, Bert White. I'm fed up with the way he always tries to
   _____ and put the blame on one of us when the boss finds
   something wrong with the section's work."

   donner tort à d'autres　　　　　　*echarle la culpa a otro*　　　　　　*place the blame or*
   responsibility on
   someone else

STOP PASSING THE BUCK!

2. "What's the crisis, Jean-Guy? I hear everyone in your Policy and Planning Section has to work overtime every night this week."
   "Oh, the usual story. Some of the higher-ups are scared we won't meet the deadline for the annual report so they (1) _____ and decided the whole section will have to work every night until the report is ready."
   "But surely you could have done it in regular working hours?"
   "Not really. We've got a pile of other rush jobs to do so we're absolutely (2)_____ _____ with work."
   "Come off it, Jean-Guy. Work! You people in Policy and Planning don't know what the word means. Now if you were in operations . . ."

   (1) ils ont pris panique   *(1) se han asustado; se asustaron*   *(1) became very frightened or excited*

   (2) débordés de   *(2) cargados*   *(2) overloaded*

3. "It's high time somebody _____ the crew in the mail room. They're always goofing off."
   "Well, I'm not going to be the one who reports them to the boss. It's not my job."

   mettre un terme à leurs activités   *acuse; informe sobre el comportamiento*   *reported their behaviour to someone in authority*

4. "Hello, Debbie. How come you're still here? I thought you were going off to head up a new section."

"I was supposed to, but the new organization chart hasn't been approved yet. It was submitted to the Management Committee but some of the directors have apparently raised some objections."

"So the reorganization isn't definite yet?"

"No, it's still _____."

incertain; en suspens   *en el aire; inseguro*   *uncertain; undecided*

5. "I've had it with those people in the Finance section. Every time I call them I get the runaround."

"Why don't you deal with the Financial Advisor, Susan Taylor? I find her very helpful."

"Well, I don't. She's the one I have the most trouble with. So help me, if I have any more hassles from her I'm going to (1) _____ and take my questions to the Director of Finance."

"I wouldn't do that if I were you. You know you just cause more trouble if you don't go through the proper channels."

"There you go again! '(2) _____.' I'm sick of people telling me not to upset the system. When the system is this bad it should be upset."

(1) sauter par dessus;
passer par dessus

(2) ne bousculez pas l'establishment;
ne poussez pas grand-mère
dans les orties

1) ir donde

2) no busques problemas

(1) go to a higher
authority than the
person in question

(2) don't cause trouble

THEN HE WENT OVER MY HEAD!

6. "Believe it or not I have something good to say about the bureaucracy for once."
"Will wonders never cease! What happened?"
"Remember I told you I needed to get a new passport for my trip to Europe? Well, I forgot to apply for it until the day before my flight."
"Oh no! What did you do?"
"Well, I took my papers and went to the passport office and explained it all to the lady at the counter. She was very sympathetic and took me to one of the higher-ups and, to make a long story short, he managed to _____ and get me a new passport in a matter of hours instead of the usual two weeks."

couper court aux formalités

acortar los trámites

shorten official procedures

7. "Hey, Bill, how come Barry's still around. Wasn't he fired? You told me they
   (1) _____."
   "They did but one of the directors
   (2) _____
   and got him reinstated."
   "Hmm. So old Barry's got friends in high places, eh? I'd better be careful what I say to him from now on."

   (1) lui ont donné son congé

   (2) a tiré les ficelles

   (1) lo despidieron; lo corrieron

   (2) usó su influencia; palanqueó

   (1) fired him

   (2) used influence

   Answers on page 87.

LOOKS LIKE WOODY'S GETTING THE AXE TODAY.

SECTION 15

Winning or Losing

THEY REALLY PULLED IT OFF!

a. are in the running
b. have the inside track
c. doesn't stand a chance
d. a shoo-in
e. take a back seat to
f. pull it off
g. got off on the wrong foot
h. on the skids
i. won hands down
j. it's a toss-up

Fill in the blanks with the best idiom from the list above.
Use the equivalents below each context in making your choice.

1. "Did you watch the debate on TV last night?"
   "Yeah. It was quite a show. Who do you think was the winner?"
   "No question about it. René _____."
   "I agree he probably won but not by that much. I thought it was pretty close."

   a gagné haut la main   *ganó de lejos*   *won easily*

2. Ted: "Who do you think will get the Assistant Director General's position?"
   Roger: "I don't even know who's being considered."
   Ted: "They say Roberts, Tremblay, Anderson and McKay (1) _____."

Alice: "Well, I'd say you can strike Roberts from the list. He (2) _____
_____ ."

Ted: "What makes you say that?"

Alice: "Because from the day he joined he hasn't gotten along with the Director General.
Poor guy. He just (3) _____ and you know how
important first impressions are to the D.G."

Roger: "Yeah, I know what you mean."

Ted: "And McKay's out of the running too. He's gone as high as he can go. In fact, I've heard
through the grapevine that they've been looking for a shelf to put him on."

Roger: "Yeah. I've heard that too. He's (4) _____ . The only
direction he's going is down."

Alice: "So it looks like Anderson and Tremblay have a better chance than the others."

Ted: "Yeah, I'd say they (5) _____ . And they're pretty evenly
matched. Either of them would make a good A.D.G. I'd say (6) _____
_____ between Anderson and Tremblay."

Alice: "I'd put my money on Anderson. She's really got what it takes. I think she's
(7) _____ ."

Roger: "Don't underestimate Tremblay. He is really sharp and very competent. He'd be my
choice."

(1) sont en lice	(1) están en la lista	(1) are being considered as candidates
(2) n'a aucune chance	(2) no tiene posibilidad ninguna	(2) has no chance of winning
(3) est parti du mauvais pied; a eu un faux départ	(3) empezó mal; comenzó mal	(3) began badly
(4) sur la pente	(4) yendo para abajo	(4) going down; failing
(5) sont tous deux favoris	(5) están en mejor posicíon	(5) are more favourably placed
(6) leurs chances sont égales	(6) están empatados	(6) their chances are equal
(7) donné gagnant	(7) el seguro ganador	(7) a sure winner; certain to win

3. "Hey, did you hear?   Maureen Marchand's been appointed head of marketing."
   "Well, well! Sam isn't going to like that."
   "You can say that again. He's been acting head for so long that he isn't going to like having to
   _____ somebody else."
   "No, he's never enjoyed playing second fiddle — and especially not to a woman."

   être le second violon   *ceder el lugar a*   *be second to;*
                                                                             be subordinate to

4. "I'm afraid we've probably lost the Melson contract. They're not happy with the last series of commercials we did for them."
"So I hear. But it's not lost yet. I've sent André to try and talk them into giving us another chance.
"Well, if anybody can persuade them, it's him."
"Yeah, my money's on André. I'm sure he can _____ ."

réussir le coup   *lograrlo*   *succeed in the face of difficulties*

Answers on page 87.

TEST 3

Based on Sections 11-15

This is a test of some of the idiomatic expressions which you met in sections 11-15.

Since this is a review the contexts are shorter and there are only English equivalents given for each item.

The exact number of words required is indicated each time by the number of blanks.

You should be able to get at least 15 out of 20 correct the first time through. If you get fewer than 15 correct you should review sections 11-15.

The answers are on page 87.

ARE IN THE RUNNING

1.
"Come on. Get to the point. ____ ____ ____ ____ ____ . I want a straight answer to my question."

don't avoid the question

2.
"Your argument is completely irrelevant. It's ____ ____ ____ ."

is not on the subject

3.
"Has a final decision been made on the proposed move yet?"
"No, they haven't decided. It's still ____ ____ ____ ____ ."

undecided

4.
"Why can't we have a four-day work week?"
"The ____ ____ is the clause in our collective agreement that specifies the hours of work."

problem point

5.
"You've got your socks on wrong. They're ____ ____ ."

the inside is turned outside

6.
"I'd say Linda ____ ____ ____ ."
"Aw, come on! I agree she won but not by that much."

won by a large number

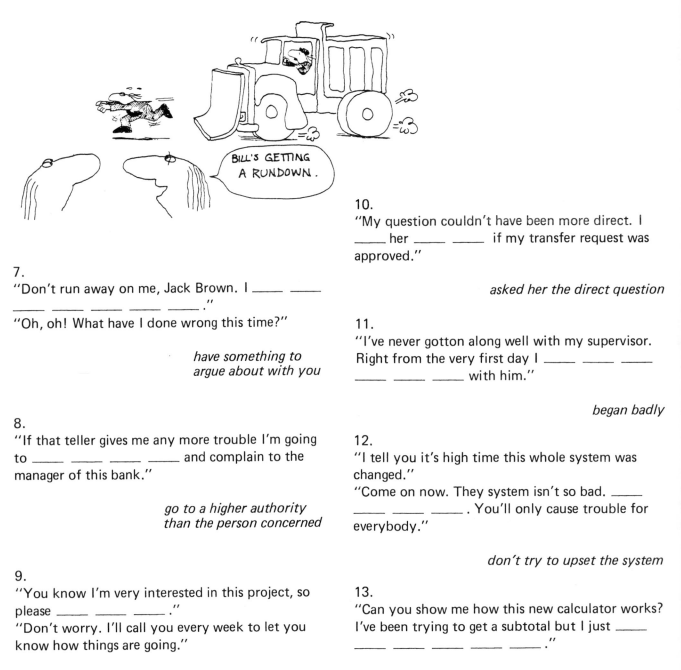

BILL'S GETTING A RUNDOWN.

7.

"Don't run away on me, Jack Brown. I ＿＿ ＿＿
＿＿ ＿＿ ＿＿ ＿＿ ＿＿."

"Oh, oh! What have I done wrong this time?"

*have something to
argue about with you*

8.

"If that teller gives me any more trouble I'm going
to ＿＿ ＿＿ ＿＿ ＿＿ and complain to the
manager of this bank."

*go to a higher authority
than the person concerned*

9.

"You know I'm very interested in this project, so
please ＿＿ ＿＿ ＿＿."

"Don't worry. I'll call you every week to let you
know how things are going."

give me any new information

10.

"My question couldn't have been more direct. I
＿＿ her ＿＿ ＿＿ if my transfer request was
approved."

asked her the direct question

11.

"I've never gotten along well with my supervisor.
Right from the very first day I ＿＿ ＿＿ ＿＿
＿＿ ＿＿ ＿＿ with him."

began badly

12.

"I tell you it's high time this whole system was
changed."

"Come on now. They system isn't so bad. ＿＿
＿＿ ＿＿ ＿＿ . You'll only cause trouble for
everybody."

don't try to upset the system

13.

"Can you show me how this new calculator works?
I've been trying to get a subtotal but I just ＿＿
＿＿ ＿＿ ＿＿ ＿＿ ＿＿ ."

don't know how to make it work

14.

"I ____ ____ ____ your remark that my theory is full of holes. In fact, I have it on good authority that it's valid."

find fault with

15.

"I'd say Tom and Helen have an equal chance of winning the chess tournament."
"I agree ____ ____ ____ between them."

their chances are equal

16.

"Just give me a rough estimate."
"Well, ____ ____ ____ ____ ____ ____ I'd say it'll cost about sixty thousand."

I guess, from memory

17.

"He won't accept blame or responsibility for anything. He always tries to ____ ____ ____ ."

put the blame or responsibility on others

18.

"The other candidates are much better qualified than Stan. He ____ ____ ____ ____ of winning."

doesn't have the possibility

19.

"If he thinks I'm going to accept such poor quality work he ____ ____ ____ a bad shock."

is certain to get

I'M AFRAID YOUR ARGUMENT DOESN'T HOLD WATER.

20.

"____ ____ ____ , Judith! You're talking nonsense."

don't talk nonsense; stop being silly

A TOSS UP

ANSWERS

SECTION 3
1. (g) see eye to eye
2. (f) rings a bell
3. (a) on the same wave-length
4. (j) knows it like the back of his hand
5. (h) heard it through the grapevine
6. (c) put your finger on it
7. (d) straight from the horse's mouth
8. (e) put two and two together
9. (b) knows the ropes
10. (i) took the words right out of my mouth

SECTION 4
1. (h) went to pieces
2. (a) was a flop
3. (g) haven't got a leg to stand on
4. (b) missed the boat
5. (c) bit off more than he can chew
6. (i) drew a blank
7. (j) on the rocks
8. (e) got out of hand
9. (d) caught red-handed
10. (f) on the blink

SECTION 5
1. (f) calling the shots
2. (d) going over big
3. (h) came out ahead
4. (i) get a load of
5. (b) in the bag
6. (c) snowballed
7. (g) made quite a name for herself
8. (a) kill two birds with one stone
9. (e) turns me on
10. (j) got it made

TEST 1 ANSWERS
1. beats me
2. high time
3. rings a bell
4. turns me on
5. went over big
6. getting out of hand
7. bit off more than I can chew
8. on the blink
9. kill two birds with one stone
10. couldn't get a word in edgewise
11. was a flop
12. slipped my mind
13. once in a blue moon
14. in no time flat
15. in the long run
16. through the grapevine
17. get a load of
18. straight from the horse's mouth
19. can't make heads or tails of
20. haven't got a leg to stand on

SECTION 1
1. (b) every now and then
2. (g) in the long run
3. (e) just in the nick of time
4. (h) on the double
5. (d) once in a blue moon
6. (f) in no time flat
7. (a) right off the bat
8. (c) it's high time
9. (j) out of the blue
10. (i) for the time being

SECTION 2
1. (g) I've lost my train of thought
2. (b) I haven't got a clue
3. (c) can't make heads or tails of
4. (i) couldn't get a word in edgewise
5. (a) slipped my mind
6. (d) on the tip of my tongue
7. (e) don't know which end is up
8. (f) beats me
9. (j) are over my head
10. (h) racking my brains

SECTION 6

1. (b) sell like hot cakes
2. (f) penny pincher
3. (d) what a rip-off
4. (j) cut corners
5. (i) corner the market
6. (e) flat broke
7. (a) in the red
8. (g) can't make ends meet
9. (h) cost you an arm and a leg
10. (c) foot the bill

SECTION 7

1. (1) (a) the last straw
   (2) (h) laying it on thick
2. (d) we're splitting hairs
3. (f) making a mountain out of a molehill
4. (b) I've had it with
5. (e) the tail wagging the dog
6. (i) pretty farfetched
7. (j) got carried away
8. (1) (g) to add insult to injury
   (2) (c) that takes the cake

SECTION 8

1. (f) find a happy medium
2. (a) make allowances for
3. (c) give him a break
4. (b) meet them halfway
5. (d) take what he says with a grain of salt
6. (h) bend over backwards
7. (e) sits on the fence
8. (j) sleep on it
9. (g) let sleeping dogs lie
10. (i) heads or tails

SECTION 9

1. (e) get away with murder
2. (1) (d) goofs off
   (2) (a) pull the wool over other people's eyes
3. (f) that's hitting below the belt
4. (c) pay lip service to
5. (1) (j) isn't pulling his (own) weight
   (2) (g) talk behind his back
6. (i) get the runaround
7. (h) taking her for granted
8. (b) a stab in the back

SECTION 10

1. (d) feeling under the weather
2. (j) speak of the devil
3. (f) put my foot in it
4. (e) have a night out on the town
5. (a) thanks all the same
6. (c) talking shop
7. (g) giving a housewarming party
8. (h) isn't it a small world
9. (1) (b) I don't feel up to
   (2) (i) can I take a rain check

TEST 2 ANSWERS

1. can't make ends meet
2. making a mountain out of a molehill
3. take (what she says) with a gain of salt
4. was the last straw
5. talking shop
6. pulling his (own) weight
7. selling like hot cakes
8. pay lip service to
9. can I take a rain check
10. what a rip-off
11. sits on the fence
12. bend over backwards
13. got the runaround
14. isn't it a small world
15. pull the wool over other people's eyes
16. cut corners
17. farfetched
18. splitting hairs
19. put my foot in it
20. find a happy medium

SECTION 11
1. (e) speak off the cuff
2. (d) asked him point blank
3. (j) don't beat around the bush
4. (a) read between the lines
5. (b) keep me posted
6. (i) drop you a line
7. (1) (f) give me a rundown
   (2) (c) off the top of my head
8. (h) spilled the beans
9. (g) off the record

SECTION 12
1. (g) inside out
2. (c) in a rut
3. (d) can't get the hang of it
4. (a) stumbling block
5. (h) upside down
6. (i) is in for
7. (j) scraping the bottom of the barrel
8. (e) in a bind
9. (f) going around in circles
10. (b) have to start from scratch

SECTION 13
1. (i) putting the cart before the horse
2. (c) have a bone to pick with you
3. (1) (g) come off it
   (2) (a) beside the point
   (3) (e) doesn't hold water
   (4) (f) take exception to
4. (b) barking up the wrong tree
5. (h) is at odds with
6. (j) that's all very well and good but
7. (d) so what?

SECTION 14
1. (d) pass the buck
2. (1) (h) pushed the panic button
   (2) (g) snowed under
3. (f) blew the whistle on
4. (b) up in the air
5. (1) (j) go over her head
   (2) (a) don't rock the boat
6. (c) cut through the red tape
7. (1) (i) gave him the axe
   (2) (e) pulled strings

SECTION 15
1. (i) won hands down
2. (1) (a) are in the running
   (2) (c) doesn't stand a chance
   (3) (g) got off on the wrong foot
   (4) (h) on the skids
   (5) (b) have the inside track
   (6) (j) it's a toss-up
   (7) (d) a shoo-in
3. (e) take a back seat to
4. (f) pull it off

TEST 3 ANSWERS
1. don't beat around the bush
2. beside the point
3. up in the air
4. stumbling block
5. inside out
6. won hands down
7. have a bone to pick with you
8. go over his/her head
9. keep me posted
10. asked (her) point blank
11. got off on the wrong foot
12. don't rock the boat
13. can't get the hang of it
14. take exception to
15. it's a toss-up
16. off the top of my head
17. pass the buck
18. doesn't stand a chance
19. is in for
20. come off it